John P. Jackson

The Bayreuth of Wagner

John P. Jackson

The Bayreuth of Wagner

ISBN/EAN: 9783337386702

Printed in Europe, USA, Canada, Australia, Japan

Cover: Foto ©ninafisch / pixelio.de

More available books at **www.hansebooks.com**

THE BAYREUTH OF WAGNER

BY
JOHN P. JACKSON

ILLUSTRATED.

NEW YORK
JOHN W. LOVELL COMPANY
150 WORTH ST., COR. MISSION PLACE

COPYRIGHT, 1891,
BY
UNITED STATES BOOK COMPANY

LIST OF ILLUSTRATIONS.

Richard Wagner—taken in 1878,	Frontispiece
Birdseye view of Bayreuth	Page 6
Map of Bayreuth	" 9
Pleasure Grounds of the Hermitage	" 13
Interior of Old Opera House	" 15
Castle and Grounds of the Fantasie	" 22
Rollwenzel House, where Jean Paul wrote	" 27
Jean Paul Richter	" 29
Jean Paul's writing room in Rollwenzel House	" 30
Jean Paul's first residence in Bayreuth	" 31
Jean Paul's Monument	" 33
Jean Paul's Statue	" 35
King Ludwig II. of Bavaria	" 40
Interior of Opera House	" 43

Franz Liszt	Page 45
Bayreuth Opera House	" 50
Opera House, Bayreuth—King's Entrance	" 52
Soiree at Wahnfried	" 53
Wagner in his "Walther" Costume	" 55
Wagner's Library at Wahnfried	" 56
The Market Place in Bayreuth	" 58
Wahnfried	" 60
An Evening with Wagner	" 63
Wagner, last picture taken, 1883	" 64
Wagner's Birthplace in Leipsic	" 67
Palazzo Vendramin, Venice	" 69
The Funeral Procession through Bayreuth	" 71
Wagner's Grave	" 72

THE BAYREUTH OF WAGNER.

THE present year will see a new pilgrimage of musical people to the ancient capital of Franconia, the home of the "Music of the Future," and the site of the Nibelung Theatre. Distant about three hours by rail from Nuremberg, Bayreuth is situated in the northeastern corner of Bavaria. It is a quiet little city of scarcely twenty thousand inhabitants, and before the year 1872 was rarely visited by tourists; indeed people had almost forgotten that such a city existed within the boundaries of the German empire; and when Wagner first announced his intention of making there a home for the "Music of the Future," several French and more than one English newspaper displayed a not inexcusable ignorance when they informed their readers that the great composer had finally decided to banish himself and his music to Beyroot, in Syria!

The history of Bayreuth may be embraced in a few paragraphs. The Hohenzollerns in their progress "Vom Fels zum Meer," touched

BIRD'S-EYE VIEW OF BAYREUTH.

the old Brandenburg Margraviate of Bayreuth-Ansbach; the forefathers of the present Emperor of Germany proceeded thence westward; and here the White Lady of this royal house still goes on her mysterious wanderings. The older portion of the city is mentioned in documents of the twelfth century. In the year 1400 it had a population of scarcely two thousand souls. In

1438 it was beleaguered by the Hussites. It suffered frequently from fire and pestilence, especially from the latter, in the years 1495, 1533, 1534, 1585, 1595, 1602, 1634, in which year nearly two thousand persons were carried off. It suffered severely during the Thirty Years' War, and was twice plundered by command of Wallenstein, in 1632 and 1634. Afterward we are told that the city was made so desolate that "wolves lurked within the city walls." Still greater trials did the city suffer on its defence of the outlawed Margrave Albrecht Alcibiades against the confederated cities, when citizen Christopher Sturm fought at the head of the guild of weavers until compelled by hunger to capitulate, and the place was given up to pillage and the flames.

Then the city came under imperial administration, and on March 27, 1557, received a lawful agnate, Margrave George Frederick, of Onolzbach, the first of the line of rulers who did so much for Bayreuth. He made the commencement and built the old castle, which was for a long time the residence of the margraves, and wherein the last scion of the house of Brandenburg-Bayreuth—Elisabeth Frederika Sophia, Duchess of Wurtemberg, died. The old structure was almost completely destroyed by fire in 1753. It is still a strong, stately edifice, marked by a peculiar octagonal tower, and is at present used for government offices. George Frederick's successor, Margrave Christian Ernst, who aided Max Emanuel against the Turks, surrounded the city with new walls and ravelins, and built a gymnasium. Christian Ernst's successor, the luxury-loving George William, turned his attention more to beautifying the city and the surroundings, and he built one of the most interesting palaces there, and transformed a large, shallow sheet of water that existed in the suburb of St. George into a large, navigable lake. He had a ship built by a local carpenter, Ruckdeschel of Muenschberg by name, and this specimen pleasing the prince so well, he ordered other vessels to be constructed, which should bear cannon and afford accommodation for crews. The largest vessel of the flotilla was a hundred feet long, twenty-two feet wide, had masts sixty feet high, bore twelve cannon, and was manned "by a large crew." With these toys the prince and the Bayreuth court amused themselves. In 1749, on the occasion of a great birthday festival, all the grand paraphernalia of lake and fleet were called into

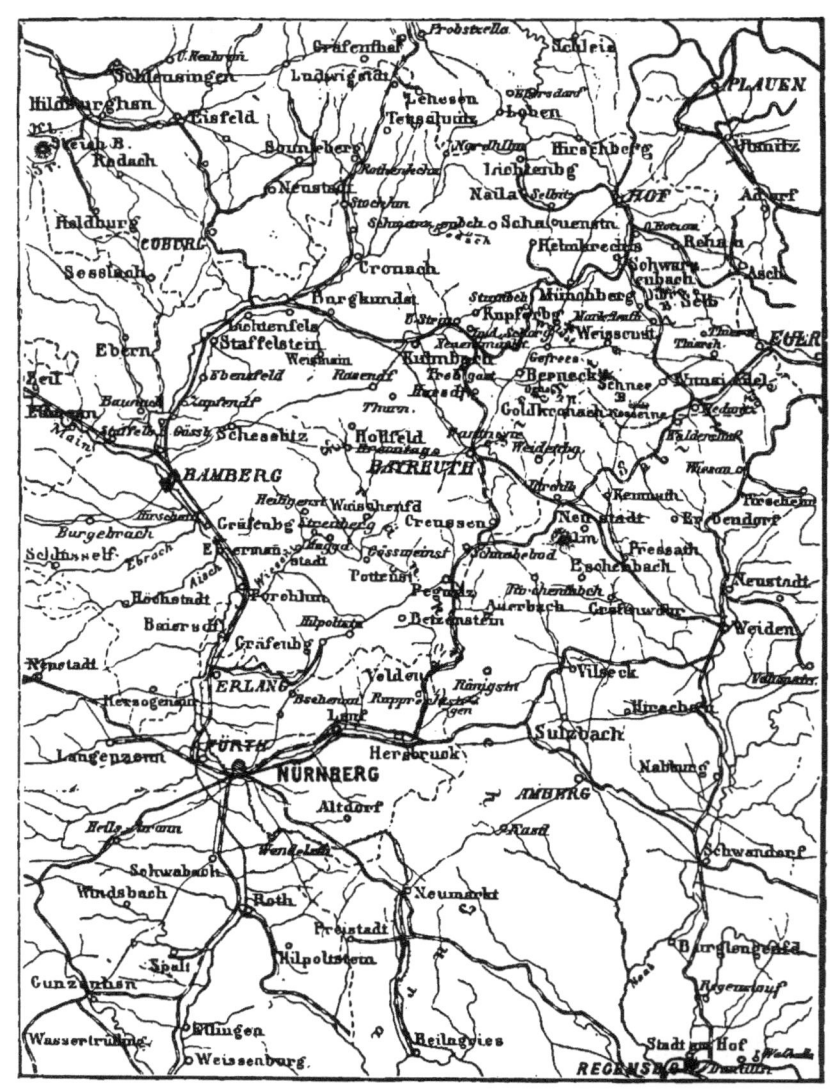

BAYREUTH.

requisition. History tells us that on this memorable occasion a "sea-fight" took place which lasted until three o'clock of the following morning, when the largest ship of the fleet caught fire, causing a loss of fifteen thousand florins. In 1755 the lake was dried up and transformed into fields and meadows—an event commemorated in verse by a local slater who had succeeded in placing a weather vane on a church steeple of St. George's:

"The Brandenburger Lake, which once much fish did yield,
We see transformed to meadow and to fruitful field;
We thank Thee, Lord and God, who o'er us ruleth well—
For all about us doth of Thy great goodness tell!"

Bayreuth's period of splendor falls in the reign of Margrave Frederick (1735-65), Margravine Wilhelmine's husband. The two entertained the idea of making Bayreuth a miniature Versailles, and they accomplished much with their annual expenditure of fifty thousand florins for monumental structures and beautifying the city. Most of the important edifices of the city date from their time. They built the new castle, the ornamental fountain in front, the beautiful opera-house, and when the Margrave died the city produced the impression of a true "city of princes," and Frederick the Great complimented his brother by telling him that "he was unable to imitate him," even with Sans Souci. In the days of Frederick the city must have presented a luxuriant appearance, when the numerous castles and palaces were inhabited, when lights blazed from hundreds of windows every night; when the court held its numerous festivals, and the Italian opera and French drama were cultivated—to say nothing of the palaces, gardens, and waterworks of the Hermitage, which cost over a million of dollars.

So many visitors did the Bayreuth court have, that Frederick felt the necessity of building a new castle for their reception, and so Das neue Schloss in the Ludwigs-Strasse was built in 1753, which was only used for the reception of passing princes and royalty. On May 13, 1812, and on August 13, 1813, Napoleon I. lodged in it, when passing with his troops through the city. It is a roomy old palace, but gloomy enough, both outside and in, and is connected with a fine park at the rear, which is now a beautiful promenade for the citizens of Bayreuth. On the large square in front is a fountain, chiefly interesting for the curious character of its water monsters. Four figures are said to symbolically represent the four rivers rising in the Fichtelgebirge—the Main, the Raab, the Saale, and the Eger—but wherein the symbolism consists it is difficult to say, and the local guide-books do not help us out. The figure on horseback represents one of the valiant ancestral margraves—Christian Ernst—who died in the year 1712. Under the horse's hoofs lies a vanquished Turk—a reference to the heroic deeds of said Margrave against the Turks in 1683. Beside the horse is the statue of this Margrave's favorite dwarf, who in the year 1714 was killed by falling off his horse.

With Margrave Frederick William, who died in 1769, the Bayreuth line of rulers ceased to exist. The land then fell to the related house of Ansbach. On December 22, 1791, Margrave Alexander of Ansbach ceded the government and land of Bayreuth to Prussia, in lieu of an annual pension. From 1806 to 1810 the margraviate was under French rule, and then it was transferred by France to the kingdom of Bavaria. From the 1st to the 4th of July, 1860, the fiftieth anniversary of this event was celebrated at Bayreuth amid great festivities. The King and Queen of Bavaria were present. To the former, Maximilian II., a monument of bronze had been erected, and this was uncovered on the first day of the festivities. On the second day there was a grand Volksfest at Buergerreuth, a prettily situated pleasure-place about half an hour's distance from the city. The great attraction was a procession, composed of twelve peasant wagons, one from each district of the circuit, each attended by peasants clad in their primitive characteristic costumes. Great interest was excited by the peasants of the Mistlegau, called there the Hummelbauern, when they executed their characteristic dance before the King and Queen. The Bayreuthers are still loyal Bavarians. They barely escaped being "annexed," however, by Prussia, after Bavaria's defeat in 1866; but Bismarck chose rather to make of King Ludwig a friend than to embitter him by taking away a rich portion of his territory. So much for the outlines of Bayreuth's history.

For the modern visitor to Bayreuth the most interesting structure is undoubtedly the old opera-house, with which we bridge over the interval from the past to the present, from the extravagant dramatic and operatic era of the mar-

PLEASURE GROUNDS OF THE HERMITAGE.

graves to the national music-drama of Richard Wagner. About the time when the Brandenburg fleet ruled the lake of St. George the Royal Opera-House was built by Margrave Frederick in the year 1748. The theatre is for the artist a gem of the Renaissance; for the culture-historian interesting on account of the position it occupies in the development, or rather the decay, of German dramatic and operatic art — for when this theatre flourished French comedy and Italian opera ruled the German court stages almost entirely. The exterior of the structure is plain and substantial; the interior surprises us with its extravagances, its excess of gilt and gilded figures. It has three rows of boxes, and is capable of holding about a thousand persons. The court-box was in the centre and was overburdened with gilt and gold-lace curtains. The theatre was so constructed that the Margrave's carriage could be driven inside the edifice and clear up to the court-box. As soon as the prince took his seat, the musicians and buglers stationed in the herald's boxes, on either side of the proscenium, gave him a blast of welcome. In a gallery extending underneath the first row of boxes, a company of the

Margrave's body-guard stood in immovable array during the entire performance.

The old Bayreuth chroniclers furnish us with some curiously interesting information about the festal performances given in this theatre on state occasions. On May 16, 1752, the birthday of the reigning Margrave, we are told that an opera entitled "Deucalion et Pyrrha" was given. The commencement was a ballet of giants, who carried large blocks of [cloth] stone to a heap and built thus a mountain. Not content with this feat the giants then carried large stones to the top of the mountain and slung them at the heavens. The gods grew angry at the impudence of the giant race. A thunderstorm gathered about the summit of the mountain, the lightning descended, and mountain and giants were destroyed, both sinking into the bowels of the earth. Then a large, brilliant cloud appeared, on which the gods sat. Then followed a smaller one, with Jupiter, Mercury, and Cupid. Venus, represented by a favorite singer—Maria Turcotto—descended from heaven in the midst of a large mass of "particularly brilliant" clouds.

When Frederic the Great was in Bayreuth, in June, 1754, a new opera, entitled "L'huomo" was

INTERIOR OF OLD OPERA HOUSE.

given "with unparalleled grandeur," at an expense to the court of twenty thousand florins—a sum which seems insignificant, however, if we consider the cost of producing modern opera. The era of dramatic and operatic extravagance ceased with the life of Margrave Frederick. When Napoleon I. was at Bayreuth he was captivated with the appearance of the brilliant little theatre, and as a memento carried with him to Paris the drop curtain—said to have been a masterpiece of art. The stage was of very large proportions—being a hundred and ten feet deep, eighty-four feet broad, and forty-two feet wide at the proscenium. The size has since then been greatly reduced. The theatre is now used only during a few months of the year, when the court dramatic company from Gera, or the Coburg opera troupe give a limited number of performances.

When Wagner first visited Bayreuth, in 1871, he had an idea that he could make use of the old opera-house for his performances of the "Ring of the Nibelungs," but on examination he found it totally unfit for his purposes. The beautiful surroundings of the city, however, so charmed him that he at once exclaimed, "Here is the site for the Nibelung Theatre!" Situated on the Red Main, in the midst of a broad and fruitful valley, to the north and east the summits of the Fichtelgebirge, to the south friendly wooded hills, certainly Richard Wagner could not have chosen for his guests a city with more delightful surroundings.

The first thing a Bayreuther will ask you is: "Have you seen the castles and parks of Fantaisie and Hermitage?" In the latter we are transported amid the memories of the luxurious, ease-loving, extravagant past; at the former we find a natural paradise, where artificial ornamentation completes, but does not increase, the charm. The palace and park of Fantaisie is a good hour's walk from the city, is reached after passing the cemetery and the bridge, either by way of the linden alley up the hill, or along the valley to the lake at the foot of the palace. The valley is one of the most charming, secluded bits of earth imaginable—"a vale of pleasure, and roses and flowers," as Jean Paul called it. He styled Hermitage the second heaven in the vicinity of Bayreuth, "for," he said, "Fantaisie is the first, and the whole country around is the third."

Jean Paul has described the beauties of the

valley leading to the Fantaisie in all moods and colors. Thus he describes it in the poetical garb of night: "What a sparkling world! Through branches and through fountains, over mountains and over woods, flowed flashing the molten veins of silver, which the moon had separated from the dross of night. Her silver glance glided over the broken wave and the trembling, smooth apple-leaf, and closely embraced the white marble pillars and the shining birch-tree stems. The lovers stood still before they entered the magic valley, as into an enchanted cavern, playing with Night and Light, into which all the fountains of life, which in the daytime had thrown up sweet odors, and voices and songs, and transparent and feathery wings, had now again fallen back and filled a deep, silent gulf." Then he describes the valley in its morning dress: "Fermian entered alone into the valley, as into a holy, mysterious temple. Every bush seemed to him transfigured by light, the brook as if flowing from Arcadia, and the whole valley spread open to him as a transplanted vale of Tempe."

And this poetic picture does not by any means overdraw the natural beauties of the valley leading to the Fantaisie, of the charming scene of wooded vale and mount, of murmuring brook and of the artificial beauties of lawn and lake. The palace and park of the Fantaisie are now the property of Duke Alexander of Wurtemberg, a liberal-minded prince who enjoys the beauties of nature and is willing to permit others less favorably situated to participate. The palace was originally built in the year 1758, and five years afterward was presented by Margrave Frederic Christian to his niece Elisabeth Frederica Sophia, who gave the park and schloss the attractive name they now bear. The palace stands on a plateau overlooking the valley and the lake, in view of a spire-crowned village on the opposite hill. The private gardens about the palace are tastefully laid out into lawns and winding and mysterious ways; and beautiful statues, among which the Amazon by Kiss, is the most interesting, are met with at almost every turn. The palace contains some noteworthy works of sculpture and painting. Near by the palace is a prettily situated hotel. In summer it is a favorite place of sojourn for strangers. On my first visit to Bayreuth Richard Wagner occupied, with his family, the upper story. Here it was where the two thousand guests who attended the ceremony of laying the foundation-stone of the Wagner Theatre, in 1872, assembled with torches and lanterns and brought the composer enthusiastic serenade.

Exactly on the opposite side of the city, and about the same distance therefrom as the Fantaisie is Jean Paul's "second heaven" of Bayreuth—the palace and park of the Hermitage. It is a delightful walk thither, under the long avenue of stately trees, where Jean Paul wandered every day to the "Rollwenzel House." "In the afternoon," says Richter, "the lovers entered the green pleasure-grounds of the Hermitage. The avenue that led to it seemed to their joyful hearts a path cut through a fragrant shrubbery. The young bird of passage, Spring, had settled upon the plains around them, and her unladen treasures of flowers lay scattered over the meadows and floated down the streams, and the birds were drawn upward by long sunbeams, and the winged world hung intoxicated in the sweet odors that were poured around." Across the fields from Frau Rollwenzel's House, and through a long and delightful lover's archway of foliage, we emerged suddenly upon the little paradise, with its fountains and lawns, and shaded walks and groves, its hermits' huts, and the curious structure called the Temple of the Sun. The latter edifice is the first to attract attention. It is a peculiar, many-sided structure, with pillars of crystal mosaic, having two wings forming a semicircle and partly embracing the large basin and fountains in front. The little temple is ornamented inside with pillars of Corinthian marble; the two side wings have fifty-eight pillars of stone mosaic, and over the capitals are heads of German emperors by Petrozzi. The edifice was built from 1749 to 1753, and is said to have cost a ton of gold. There is nothing particular to be seen in the rooms except a portrait of the supposed White Lady and her mother. The fountains in front, with curiously carved water-monsters, are weak imitations of Versailles.

The palace of the Hermitage is a remarkably plain, one-storied structure, and was commenced in 1715 by Margrave George William, whose descendants built the Temple of the Sun and the many water-fountains. The palace itself is chiefly interesting on account of the historical reminiscences connected with it, its peculiarly furnished rooms, its collections of curiosities, its frescoes and portraits. In it Margravine Wilhelmine, the sister of Frederic the Great, wrote her "Memoirs;" and in the large marble hall Margrave Frederic William founded, about the middle of the past century, the order of the Red Eagle. The portraits are especially interesting. Among them are Frederic the Great as a boy, and as regent, his father and mother, his sister Wilhelmine, Gustavus Vasa, Maria Theresa, the Empress Catharine II. of Russia, and other prominent persons. Some of the rooms are peculiarly interesting. The walls of one consist of square tablets of Chinese porcelain—relief-pictures richly inlaid with gold corns—a present to the Margravine Wilhelmine by her brother Frederic the Great. The purchase and transportation of these tablets cost the great Frederic not less than half a million of thalers. Another room is "papered," if we may use the expression, with pieces of broken looking-glass, of all sizes and shapes. This curious whim was carried out by Margrave Frederick to commemorate an act of his own carelessness. In 1763 he was sitting at his room window with a lighted candle, which he placed incautiously too near the curtains. These caught fire and a great portion of the castle was destroyed. Afterward he had all the pieces of the mirrors, which had been cast out of the window, gathered up and formed into this strange ornament. The last royal sojourners in the castle were King Max of Bavaria, in June and July, 1851, and King Otto of Greece, in 1865. The late King of Bavaria, when he visited the Hermitage, lived in one of the wings of the Temple of the Sun—certainly a fitting residence for such a poetic and musical monarch.

At every step we take in this little paradise we are reminded of the past grandeurs, of the endeavor on the part of the margraviate court to render life pleasant and to while away the *ennui* of a pampered existence. The very name of the place and the presence of a number of little hermits' huts remind us of the peculiar existence which the court led. Tired of the brilliant life and show around them, they sought amusement and excitement in playing at hermits. About the beautiful grounds they built themselves small huts, in which the members of the court dwelt during the summer months, wearing hermit's garb and doing mock penance. The Margrave was the president of the body, and called

CASTLE AND GROUNDS OF THE FANTAISIE.

his brethren together by ringing a little bell on his own hut. At certain hours of the day the ladies of the court could take part in the recreation. Thus did they seem to have grown tired of the luxuries they had created around them. The gushing fountains, the temple-like retreats, the charming walks, the graceful statues, the paintings and riches of the interior of the palaces, no longer satisfied them, and they sought pleasure in contrast. They even studied classic history for their amusement. In 1744 they built a Roman theatre, as a ruin, and while the princely audience sat under the shade of stately trees, Italian operas and French comedies were performed for their amusement. The theatre looks to-day as it must have looked a century and a quarter ago, excepting, of course, the influence of weather and time on the structure. It was open from all sides, and, scenically considered, was sufficient for the Italian operas and French plays of the times, for which but little scenery was required.

Let us transport ourselves back to the year 1743. The Margravine has distinguished visitors—her brother the victorious Frederick the Great, her brother Prince August William, and the youngest of the family, Ferdinand of Prussia. With Frederick comes, of course, Voltaire. An old picture, now at the Hermitage, represents a scene that occurred on the last day of August in the above-mentioned year. Frederick has gone to Ansbach on political business; and to amuse his favorite, Voltaire, his sister exerts all her intellect and skill, providing him with everything he can wish, and with drama or opera. The Margravine-hostess sits with her face toward him, and is engaged in conversation with several courtiers, perhaps Kayserling, her brother's favorite; perhaps her confidant and friend and body physician, Von Superville, her adviser in scientific and artistic matters, to whom later she gave the manuscript of her " Memoirs." The principal figure is Voltaire, seated in conscious dignity in his fauteuil immediately before the stage. The lady standing to his left, with her left hand caressing a poodle, is the Duchess of Wurtemberg, a woman of courageous manners and morals. To the left again of the Duchess is a young lady of the court, Fräulein Albertine von der Markwitz, the favorite of Margrave Friedrich himself, who is one of the party. The relationship of these two is still called to memory by an inscription hewn in the stone of the first inner arch of the Roman theatre: "Albertine de Markwitz, mieux gravée dans mon cœur que sur cette pierre." Such is an interesting picture of dramatic life at that time.

Margravine Wilhelmine is the true creator of most of the curious structures about the park. She even built a ruin copy of Virgil's tomb, as a monument for a dead lapdog! It is still in a pretty good state of preservation. But classicity, like religion, was with the Bayreuth court but a plaything. The Margraves are long forgotten, but the beautiful paradises they created still remain. Under the shady trees where once sat the margraviate court listening to, or rather gossiping, during the dramatic or operatic performances, now sit on Sunday afternoons the good people of Bayreuth, and drink beer and coffee in their quiet, good-natured fashion. A little chapel, wherein Margravine Wilhelmine is said to have spent much of her time in writing her "Memoirs," is now a ruin, from the centre of which a large tree spreads its foliage as a shady roof. Everywhere ruins — memories of past splendor and extravagance — everywhere the beauties of nature triumphant, justifying Jean

Paul in designating the Hermitage as Bayreuth's "second heaven." But we cannot leave the beautiful paradise without a word on the Margravine herself. Here she wrote those bright, witty, attractive "Memoirs," in which the manners and history of the past century are reflected so faithfully that the historian cannot find any better source. A portrait of the Margravine is unfortunately not found at the Hermitage; but in the Military Hospital, in the suburb of St. George (formerly the Brandenburg Schloss), there is a picture of her. She is represented as an attractive lady, with a small mouth, high forehead, and large, deep, intellectual eyes, the features strongly reminding us of those of Frederick the Great.

Memories of Jean Paul clinging to Bayreuth make the city exceedingly attractive to lovers of German literature. The places where great men have lived, where they wrote their immortal works, will always have a peculiar charm for their admirers. In Bayreuth we have everywhere pleasant reminiscences of Jean Paul Friedrich Richter, usually styled Jean Paul, one of the greatest of German humorists, the contemporary of Goethe and Schiller and Wieland.

THE ROLLWENZEL HOUSE, WHERE JEAN PAUL WROTE.

The house No. 384 Friedrichsstrasse bears the inscription: "In this house lived and died Jean Paul Friedrich Richter." Half an hour's distance from Bayreuth is a little inn, styled the "Rollwenzel House," and it bears the inscription: "Here wrote Jean Paul." Opposite the Gymnasium stands the monument to Jean Paul, modelled by Schwanthaler, and erected in the year 1841 by King Ludwig I. of Bavaria. In the cemetery is the poet's last resting-place, marked by a simple, noble monument. Indeed every important place in and around Bayreuth has memories of Jean Paul, of whom Boerne could say in his enthusiasm: "Ask ye where Jean Paul was born, where he lived, and where rest his ashes? From heaven he came, on earth he dwelt, our heart is his grave! Will ye hear of the days of his childhood, of the dreams of his youth, of his mature years? Ask the boy Gustav, ask the youth Albano, and the true-hearted Schopper. Search ye for his hopes? Ye will find them in the Campanerthal. No hero, no poet has given such truthful information of his life as Jean Paul. His life is gone; but his word remains."

Jean Paul was a native of Wunsiedel, but

the best years of his life—nearly a quarter of a century—were spent in Bayreuth, where he settled permanently after his marriage, in 1804. As a guest he had visited the city nine years earlier, and had even found a Bayreuth bookseller, named Lübeck, ready to publish one of his works. In 1795 he wrote: "Bayreuth is my valley of May." Another time he wrote: "In Bayreuth my minutes are made into rosettes, my hours into brilliants; but in proportion my memories of Hof grow up like gravestones around me." When he finally removed with his family to Bayreuth it was to him like returning home to an old circle of acquaintances. The city and the neighborhood were already familiar to him. Years before he had wandered in the beautiful valley of the Fantaisie, and in the charming park of the Hermitage, and among the neighboring mountains, pictures of which he had woven in his "Flower, Fruit, and Thorn Pieces." In the mist-world of the Fichtelgebirge he says he erected for himself a new morning-world. Nowhere could he have selected a city with surroundings better suited to his disposition. The beauties and charms of nature were necessary to inspire him. Though roughly moulded he

JEAN PAUL RICHTER.

was a lovable soul, a passionate friend of free nature, influenced and carried away by the beauty and fragrance of the world of plants, the ever-changing colors of the skies, and the manifold impressions of rural existence.

After passing the winter in the city he seemed to acquire new life and enthusiasm for labor with the return of spring. Then on every fine morning, as early as six, he might be seen wandering out beneath the noble avenue of elms to the little inn kept by his friend Frau Rollwenzel. Clad like a robust farmer, with his shirt-collar open, a satchel containing books and papers and a bottle of wine slung over his shoulder, and followed by his favorite poodle, he left his family every morning, and remained at the Rollwenzel House all day long. There he wrote and drank his wine until one; he worked again until five without further stimulant; from five to seven he drank beer and gossiped with Frau Rollwenzel, or read and made extracts for the morrow. Frau Rollwenzel felt justly proud of her distinguished guest, and always kept one of her upper rooms in good order for his use. Here, or in the little garden, or on an elevation near by, Jean Paul would sit over his beer until dusk, or until his children came to fetch him home, or until Frau Rollwenzel herself reminded him that it was time to be getting toward Bayreuth. Frau Rollwenzel's house is still standing, in the same condition as in Jean Paul's time, and the poet's work-room is kept in the state in which he left it. It is ex-

JEAN PAUL'S WRITING-ROOM IN ROLLWENZEL HOUSE.

ceedingly plainly furnished, and besides a number of manuscripts contains a portrait of Frau Rollwenzel and a portrait and bust of the poet.

Jean Paul's life in Bayreuth was pleasant to him. His first residence was over an apothecary's store on the Market-Place, in the house No. 384 Friedrichsstrasse, with his friend Von Donecke, the author of a work on "German Mediæval Folk-lore and Heroic Legends." He

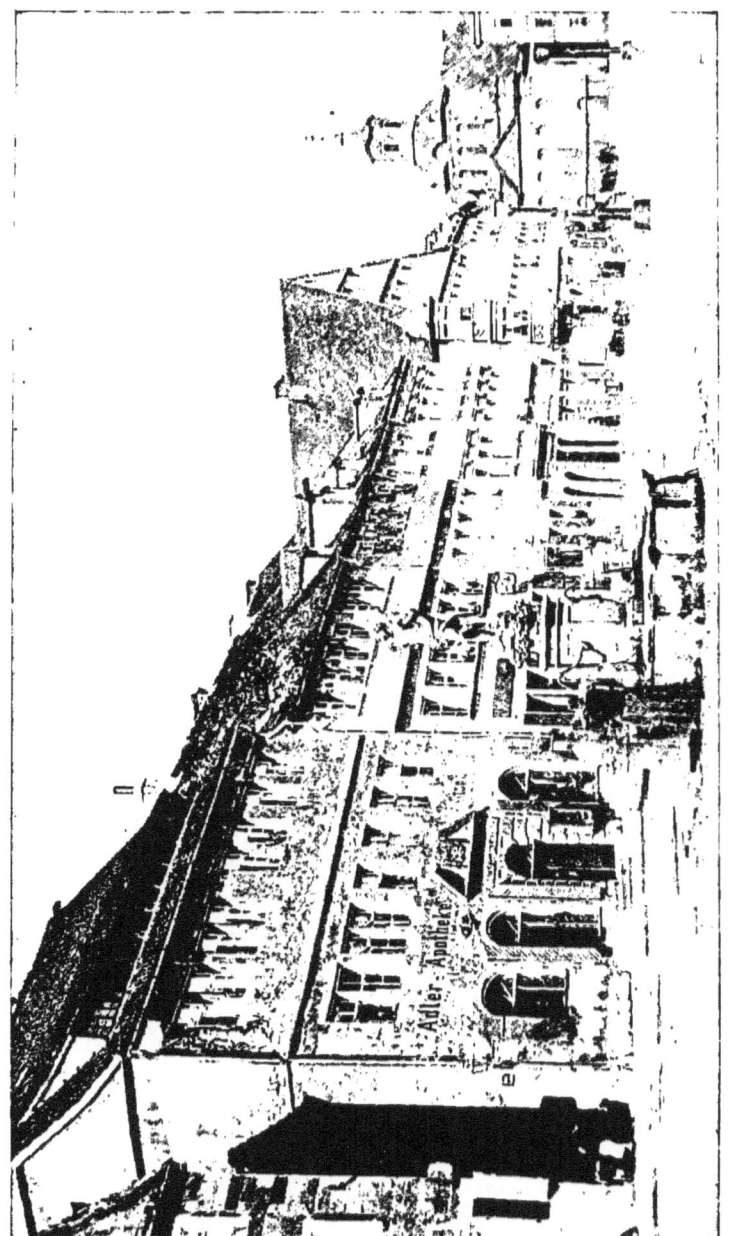

JEAN PAUL'S FIRST RESIDENCE IN BAYREUTH.

was everywhere hospitably welcomed. In the evenings he visited the Harmonie Club, where he read the newspapers, and chatted with his acquaintances. He visited the theatre, the concerts, and enjoyed the Marionette theatres at fair-times. He took an active interest in charitable affairs of the city. Once he wrote to a lady friend : "Imagine me in winter, clad in a mantle, standing near the great soup caldron (in the soup kitchen), and my dog beside me. We both try the soup—I alone deal out the portions, and am very careful about it. But, alas, the hungry, starving misery about me!"

Noted literary and princely visitors were frequently announced at Jean Paul's house. Fichte visited him in the spring of 1805, and on October 23, 1808, Varnhagen von Ense, who of course made a note of the event in his interminable "Correspondence." " Jean Paul," he says, "is a pure, noble man; no deceit, nothing mean in his life: he is just as he writes, affectionate, cordial, strong, and good. After supper he gave me his hand, saying : "Pardon me ; I must go to bed. But it is very early yet : stay, in God's name, and gossip with my wife. I am a Philistine and the hour is come when I must sleep."

In September, 1822, Friedrich Perthes, the book-dealer, visited him, and spent two evenings with him, but does not appear to have taken such agreeable impressions away with him as did Varnhagen. He says that the poet used interminable heavy sentences in his conversation, and dilated half an hour on the best means of getting to sleep. "Nothing of the quick flashes, the intellectual sparks, the excellent comparisons, the brilliant pictures of which his works are full appeared in his conversation." He describes him as a man of large, bony frame, more like a forester or a farmer than a poet. Very different was the impression made by Jean Paul on the natural philosopher Steffens, who afterward wrote to him: "Yesterday evening I revelled in the world of your imagination and of your dreams, and I was carried away by your pictures of living and dying and youth and courage."

Jean Paul wrote over half a dozen of his books while residing at Bayreuth, besides preparing an edition of his collected works. He commenced writing an autobiography in 1818, but did not get beyond the account of his boyhood. He wrote and read and made extracts partly in his own house, partly in the little room at Frau Rollwenzel's house, and partly in other favorite places which he searched out for himself. Thus before the Hermitage Gate of the

JEAN PAUL'S MONUMENT.

city he had the use at all times of Kammerrath Miedel's garden and the summer-house, from which he could command a view of the lovely Maienthal, of the suburb of St. George, of the neighborhood of the Hermitage, and of the Fichtelgebirge. Before the Friedrich's Gate the poet had a second favorite garden, belonging to Herr von Hagen, where he wrote, inspired by the charming landscape about him.

Jean Paul died on November 14, 1825. His grave in the cemetery at Bayreuth is marked by an immense block of granite, which bears, on a copper plate, the inscription:

Jean Paul Friedrich Richter,
born March 21, 1763, at Wunsiedel,
died November 14, 1825, at Bayreuth;
and his son,
Max Emanuel Richter,
born November 9, 1805, at Coburg,
died September 25, 1821, at Bayreuth.

Sixteen years afterward, on the anniversary day of his death, a bronze statue of the poet, presented to the city by King Ludwig I. of Bavaria, was uncovered with fitting ceremonies. Schwanthaler has wonderfully incorporated in the bronze the genius and character of the poet! With pencil in hand he stands before us, thoughtful and creating, as if inspired with the highest ideas of the True, the Good, and the Beautiful. The high brow announces the great mind that worked behind it; the eye, the mild, gentle character of his life; the corners of the mouth reveal to us, even in bronze, the humor,

JEAN PAUL'S STATUE.

the repose, and the earnest truthfulness that he recorded on every page of his works. Truly "his dreams were full of Springtime, and his Springtimes were full of dreams."

I.

RICHARD WAGNER's intention was originally not only to build the Nibelung Theatre, wherein should be performed his own great music dramas, but to make Bayreuth a nursery for the culture of national German opera, and the city of annual musical dramatic festivals for Germany. In his selection Wagner was influenced more perhaps by his obligation to his friend King Ludwig to erect his theatre within the boundaries of Bavaria, than to any connection of the city or neighborhood with the Nibelung legend. Had he adopted the ideas of Eduard Devrient for the founding of German dramatic festivals in Germany, he would have chosen as the site for his theatre the city of Worms, the ancient seat of the kings of Burgundy, described so minutely in the "*Nibelungenlied*," where Siegfried wooed Gudrun, after forgetting his valiant conquest of Brunnhilda in her charmed, fire-surrounded retreat, and where he received his death-wound from the grim, revengeful Hagen. The story of the Nibelungen belongs to the Rhine as much as the story of the Reformation does to Wittenberg, of St. Elizabeth to the Wartburg, of Barbarossa to the Kyffhäuser.

Wagner had in mind when he made his selection of Bayreuth not only the roomy palaces for the reception of princely guests and patrons, but the beautiful surroundings of the city. For nature was a part of Wagner's musical creed; the festal gatherings which he proposed were to be periods of esthetic enjoyment; the days were to be spent in excursions to the beautiful retreats of the vicinity; the evenings devoted to the musical-dramatic entertainments, to witnessing the beauties and grandeurs of the great German "Iliad," musically and dramatically given in its connection with Scandinavian-Teutonic mythology. On the occasion of laying the foundation-stone of the Nibelung Theatre, in 1872, he said that, if in his opera of the "Meistersinger" he had praised Nuremberg as being the centre of Germany, he would admit that Bayreuth deserved equally well that title of honor. As to the name "Bayreuth," he said the most acceptable explanation was that the Bayern or Bavarians, whose dukes received the land from the Franconian kings, had there a settlement, a *rod* or *reuth*, which signifies a "clearing," a "place wrung from the wilderness and given over to culture." The land was originally the Franconian boundary of the German empire against the hostile Czechs, some of whose more peaceful brethren had early settled near by, and had given names to settlements and villages all around. Wagner accepted the word *reuth*, therefore, in its full significance, as a clearing, a place wrung from the wilderness. So, he said, should Bayreuth become a city wrung from the wilderness of the prevailing operatic extravagances!

II.

It is not necessary at this time to tell the story of Wagner's life and the many reasons that led him finally to select Bayreuth as the site of the Nibelung Theatre. King Ludwig II., the poetic-minded monarch of Bavaria, wished that the poet-composer should take up his residence in his capital, Munich, and before the latter's banishment to Switzerland plans had been submitted to the young ruler, and approved by him, of a theatre to be built on the heights overlooking the Isar. King Ludwig tells himself, in some most charming letters which he wrote to a beautiful Bavarian girl, "Fräulein von Rebach," and which have been published in a little volume entitled "Alpenrosen und Gentianen," how he first became acquainted with Wagner through his opera of "Tannhäuser" and by reading his brochures on "The Art-Work of the Future" and "The Music of the Future."

"I read and re-read," writes the King, "and felt as if transported. Yes: so I had myself dreamt of the influence of Musical Art. From such a blending with Poetry must surely arise the completed Art-Work of the Future. And here was a man who felt within himself the power to create something so elevated and so glorious! One could feel in the words, that seemed to have poured forth from his soul like a stream of lava, that he would be able to carry out what he had set himself to do, and that he possessed the inexpressible consecration of genius through which the Ideal is enchanted into palpable reality. . . . And the wings of this heroic spirit were bound. Miserable hindrances prevented his heavenward flight, chained him to the ground! He sought a human being who had the power and the will to help him. If he could find a prince, 'sufficiently inspired by striving for the Ideal, who could understand him, with a mind grand enough to enable him to assist him with his power,' the future of his Art would be assured.

"Can you blame me, Elizabeth, when I held such words to be a call of fate addressed to me? Shortly after I heard 'Lohengrin.'

KING LUDWIG II. OF BAVARIA.

What was there lacking to complete the enchantment, after the glory of those magical strains? Having spent my boyhood in Hohenschwangau, the legend of the Swan Knight, with its irrepressible poetic magic, had, so to speak, grown into my flesh and blood. . . . On the following morning, nay, the very same night, I wrote to Richard Wagner and called him to me. My Cabinet Council sent the invitation to Lucerne and my ardent wish was quickly filled—the Poet-Composer came to Munich. How his wonderful creations, the magic of his personality, took me captive, how we became friends, friends in the highest ideal significance of this much-abused word, the world knows all. And those whom I never loved drove me more and more within myself and to the few chosen ones, because of the despicable manner in which they interpreted this friendship. What, in this respect, should I not have to experience and to endure from this venal, despicable world, if I were not King, if I dared not set my foot upon its neck as often as I wished?

"But that even my sweetest friend Elizabeth did not approve of this friendship, that she should have to warn me against this friend, filled me with pain! Will it always be so? Are there no means by which you can be drawn within this blissful, magical circle? . . . So it is from 'Tristan and Isolde' that your aversion came. I can well understand that this creation can wound and repulse a pure maidenly nature.

. . . How clever you are, Elizabeth. You compare my love for Wagner's music with my passion for the scent of the jasmine, which latter you yourself struggle against in vain. There is something related in the two: sultry and intoxicating, the one as well as the other. So it is not my friendship for Wagner that you blame, but what you call its excess, and my disposition to clothe men born of dust with divine attributes. You think with fear and trembling of Wagner's influence upon me, and still more on the impression which the waning of this friendship will make upon me. As regards the latter you are right. There is nothing to compare with such an impression. In that case something irreparable would break in my soul, and the bright sun of existence would for me be darkened. God in his grace will save me from such an event, and let me keep the joy I find in promoting and carrying out the plans of the

INTERIOR OF OPERA HOUSE.

THE BAYREUTH OF WAGNER. 43

dear friend, and to be to him in a slight measure what he is to me in so infinite a degree."

After all, the King had to let Wagner go or brave a revolution, such as his grandfather, Ludwig I., had met and succumbed to in a less pure enthusiasm. But the monarch never withdrew his favor from the great composer, and he it was who furnished nearly two hundred thousand dollars of the money wherewith the Nibelung Theatre in Bayreuth was eventually built. I was present when the foundation-stone of the structure was laid on May 22, 1872, amid great festal harmony and enjoyment. Two thousand guests, among them many of Germany's most eminent musicians and singers, had assembled at Wagner's call, and the three days' sojourn and festivities in Bayreuth will long be remembered by those who participated in them—the excursions to the charming places around the old city, the torchlight procession to the Fantaisie, where Wagner then resided, and the serenade there to the composer himself. The ceremonies connected with the laying of the foundation-stone were unfortunately marred by a pouring rain, but were nevertheless a most interesting event. After the musicians had played the Huldigungsmarsch, which the composer had written in honor of his royal patron, Wagner struck the stone thrice with the hammer, saying: "Blessed be thou, O Stone! Stand long and hold fast!" In a zinc encasement was placed a telegram received that day from the King, which read: "To the Poet-Composer, Richard Wagner, in Bayreuth: To you, dearest friend, I send, from the innermost depths of my heart, my warmest congratulations, on this day so auspicious for the whole of Germany. Blessing and success to the grand enterprise greet you. To-day I am, more than ever, united in spirit with you. (Signed) Ludwig." Among other things buried beneath the stone was a poetical enigma, written by Wagner himself, which read:

> "Hier schliess ich ein Geheimniss ein,
> Da ruh' es viele hundert Jahr!
> So lange es verwahrt der Stein,
> Macht es der Welt sich offenbar.
> RICHARD WAGNER."
> BAYREUTH, May 22, 1872.

The translation being, "A secret great I here enclose; many hundred years here let it rest; so long as the stone guards it well, to the world it will itself reveal." Then guests and musicians

FRANZ LISZT.

assembled in the old theatre of the margraviate days, to complete the ceremony which the rain had marred on Nibelung Hill. Singers and musicians filled the immense stage, and the large house was crowded with guests. In front of the singers the composer took his place, and beside him sat his wife, the daughter of Franz Liszt, surrounded by her children.* After words of welcome by the burgomaster of the city, Wagner, deeply moved, read an address in which he uttered the aims and hopes he entertained in regard to the new theatre and his grand visions of the future. "The eternal God," he exclaimed, "lives assuredly within us before we build a temple to his glory : and this temple of ours reveals externally the existence of the art-spirit within us that shall build it. Let this temple be consecrated by your love, by your blessing, by the deep thanks I feel toward you—to you all who worked for me, granted, gave, and helped. Let it be consecrated by the spirit that induced you to follow my invitation, which fills you with the courage to defy every scorn and to trust in

* Wagner's first wife died in January, 1866, after five years' separation from him, and in August, 1870, he was married to Cosima Liszt the divorced wife of Hans von Bulow.

me." With the last words Wagner raised his hands and evoked, as if by magician's wand, from the three hundred singers and musicians around him the beautiful strains of the "Wach Auf!" choral of the last act of "Die Meistersinger," to the words with which Hans Sachs, the cobbler-poet and Mastersinger of Nuremberg greeted the appearance and labors of Luther as the Wittenberg Nightingale:

> "Awake, the dawn of day is near,
> I hear singing so loud and clear,
> A wondrous throated Nightingale,
> Whose voice is heard o'er hill and dale.
> The Night sinks to the Occident,
> The Day mounts from the Orient,
> And morning's purple glories loom
> Up from the realm of night and gloom."

Wagner himself was visibly affected. He embraced his wife and children tenderly, and even the burgomaster and the banker Feustel, who stood near by. Wagner thanked his guests, and the ceremony was over. In the afternoon Wagner directed Beethoven's Ninth Symphony, the singers, Niemann, Betz, Frl. Lehmann, and Frau Jachmann-Wagner taking the leading parts. In the evening there was a banquet at the Hotel zur Sonne (renowned as the place where Jean Paul was fond of *kneiping*), when Wagner delivered a heartfelt toast to his great benefactor, King Ludwig, giving interesting scraps of autobiography.

"When I was finally permitted," he said, "to return to Germany, and the official musical institutions did not know what to do with me, the great-hearted voice which penetrated to my soul called to me and said: 'I will take care that thou, Man of Music, whom I love, whose thoughts I wish to be carried out, shall in future be freed from all material cares.'"

We know how well Ludwig kept his word. While the world at large was ridiculing Wagner and the music of the future, this young King, who was gifted with a higher, purer nature than most other European monarchs, took the composer under his wing, gave him a pension, ordered his operas to be given at his court theatre, and never afterward, till the day of the composer's death, hesitated to give him his friendship and support.

"It is a miracle," once wrote Wagner, referring to King Ludwig's friendship. "I remember a dream which I had as a youth. I dreamed that

Shakespeare was living, and that I saw him and spoke to him in person. I have never forgotten the impression which this made upon me, and which aroused in me the desire to see Beethoven (who, too, was no longer among the living). Somewhat similar must be the feelings of this young King toward me. He tells me that he can hardly believe that I am really his. His letters to me no one can read without astonishment and delight. Liszt remarked that his reciptivity, as shown in them, was on the same lofty plane as my productivity. Believe me, it is a miracle."

Poor Ludwig! On June 13, 1886, Whit-Monday, the world was startled by the news that he had committed suicide by drowning in beautiful Lake Starnberg. A royal life, that had been wonderfully beautiful in its beginning, thus came to an unexpected close. Wagner's music had exercised its enchantment upon him to the end. A strange, unfathomable seduction lurked in it. It was the musical apotheosis of love. It painted in ravishing colors the mission of humanity. Heard in the "storm-and-stress" period of humanity it surges upon its victim like a raging fire. It seized upon the King in its voluptuous, emotional magic. Ludwig could understand, but would not realize, the poetry of "Tristan and Isolde."

> "So let us here together blend,
> Living, loving, without end.
> No awaking,
> No forsaking,
> To each other mated,
> Forever consecrated."

III.

THE Nibelung Theatre was at last completed, and the first performances of "The Ring of the Nibelung" were given. That was the summer of 1876, when I had the pleasure of seeing much of the poet-composer and learning a great deal about his life and his methods of work. From sketches made at the time I may be permitted to make a few extracts. Wagner was then over sixty years of age, and though far from being majestic in personal appearance, I always felt with him that I was in the presence of an extraordinary man. In conversation he was fluent, but it was always extremely difficult to follow him in his flights of ideas, for his sentences were almost interminable, and he illustrated his remarks by comparisons and illustrations from the most abstruse realms of thought and philosophy. In Bayreuth he was monarch supreme. Inside the Festal Theatre his rule was despotic. His spirit pervaded everything and everybody, from the scene-shifter to the

BAYREUTH OPERA HOUSE.

most famous singer. At the rehearsals, seated in an armchair in a corner of the proscenium, he looked a mere speck in the landscape revealed on the stage. Every note, every bar of the instrumentation, every dramatic movement, every attitude or position of the singer upon the stage, every idea expressed in painting or music, every line of poetry, every imitation of nature's grandest effects, was the expression and work of his unaided intellect.

Permit me to quote what I wrote at the time from Bayreuth: "Suddenly something goes wrong with the scenery; he springs up from his chair, darts to the back of the scenes; you hear the stamping of feet, the sound of sharp words; but the man who returns to the front of the scene has a face calm and unruffled as before. Then a singer has to be corrected. A line or a passage is not interpreted aright, and the composer walks quietly across the stage, takes Siegfried's shield and spear, and silently shows Herr Unger the proper dramatic gesture. The composer will frequently sing and act a passage as he wishes it given, and it is an infinite pleasure to see how cheerfully such great artists as Betz, Niemann, Gura, Hill, and the rest carry out the Meister's suggestions and instruction. Nothing can escape Wagner's eye or ear. The orchestra is repeatedly stopped, and the good-natured Hans Richter looks up interrogatively from his 'mystic abyss,' otherwise called the 'conductors' grave,' where he conducts in shirt-sleeves and open vest. 'Mein lieber Richter, just repeat that passage; but the bass more subdued!' . . . 'So! Gut! Gut! that is better!' and the Meister settles down again in his chair at the corner of the stage, and the rehearsal proceeds. Take your eyes away from the stage for a while, and you will be surprised to hear a voice not far away from you in the auditorium. It is Wagner's; he is examining the perspective. After all the troubles and vexations of rehearsal are over, about seven or eight in the evening, the more genial side of Wagner's character is revealed. In the restaurant close to the theatre, a large table is reserved for the composer and his wife, his ministers or 'Verwaltungsrath,' and the principal singers. Wagner is received with royal honors, those already seated around the table rise, cigars are placed on one side for the moment, and greetings are given and received. If the Meister has

OPERA HOUSE, BAYREUTH, KING'S ENTRANCE.

SOIRÉE AT WAHNFRIED.

1, Wagner. 2, Liszt. 3, Siegfried. 4, Frau Cosima. 5, Fr. v. Lenbach. 6, E. Scaria. 7, Frau Materna. 8, Fr. Fischer. 9, Frau Brandt. 10, H. Levi. 11, Hans Richter. 12, Fr. Betz. 13, A. Niemann. 14, Gräfin, Sch. 15, Gräfin, W. 16, v. Schudowsky.

been particularly annoyed in the theatre, and hard words have been uttered, he heals at the table all wounded susceptibilities. 'Mein lieber Freund Betz,' or 'Meine liebe Frau Materna' are cordially embraced, and champagne is ordered by the Meister to drown all the recent annoyances in forgetfulness. At nine the Meister is driven home, and the artists seek the classic vaults of Angermann's, where foaming Bayrisch is handed by the gentle-faced Marie until one or two o'clock in the morning."

"More interesting than those at the theatre were the rehearsals held at Wagner's house in the year 1875, before the composer had begun to feel the burden of theatrical management, as he did in 1876. Betz, Niemann, Scaria, Unger, Schlosser, Hill, Vogl, Madame Materna, the sisters Lehmann, and others had responded to his call, and gathered during the summer of 1875 in Bayreuth, for the purpose of studying their various *rôles*. These pianoforte rehearsals lasted usually from eleven in the morning till one, and in the afternoon again from five until seven, after which "Abendessen" was announced for master and *artistes*—cold meats, salads, beer, wine, or tea; sometimes served in the dining-room, but more frequently, when the weather permitted, in the garden. Here the composer could be seen in his most genial mood; he would relate anecdotes and incidents of his student-life and early theatrical wanderings, with many a curious trait of his earlier migratory existence; and once he spoke of his courtship days and his marriage with his first wife. Occasionally he would read chapters from a bulky manuscript autobiography, which he keeps carefully stowed away somewhere in his library, for the benefit of the world when he shall be no more among the living. When the weather was unpropitious, the little company would retire to the large *salon*, and the evening would be devoted to music and singing. Wagner himself would sometimes play the pianoforte accompaniment; then, as a change, he would declaim an act from one of Shakespeare's dramas, of which he is a devoted admirer. Once he promised to read his poem of "Parsifal," the subject of his forthcoming opera, but something interfered to prevent this. Many a singer looks back with pleasure on the days spent in Bayreuth during the '75 rehearsals, and the evening gatherings in the *salon* and garden of the Villa Wahnfried. In ordinary times, when the singers are not assembled round the master, Bayreuth and the Villa Wahnfried are very quiet places indeed."

Wagner was an early riser and a hard worker.

WAGNER IN HIS "WALTHER" COSTUME—HIS FAVORITE DRESS WHEN AT WORK.

The young secretaries, Mottl and Seidl, who assisted him to prepare his scores, could tell interesting stories of the poet-composer's life. When writing the "Goetterdaemmerung" he was up at five o'clock in the summer and six in the winter. He began work at once, and did not allow himself to be interrupted till two in the afternoon, by which time the floor would be strewn half an inch thick with manuscript. Sometimes for days at a time he would not put pen to paper until he felt the inspiration to work

WAGNER'S LIBRARY AT WAHNFRIED.

again. He usually wrote in the grand salon of Villa Wahnfried, where the light and sunshine and fresh air could enter without hindrance. During the periods of his mental repose he would rise at a later hour and pass the day idly, reading his letters and looking after his dogs and his chickens. Dinner was at one, and from three to four was devoted to sleep, and then, after a cup of coffee, he would take his two big Newfoundland dogs and wander either along the avenue of linden-trees to the Rollwenzel House, or across the fields to the little paradise of the Hermitage, or to the castle and park of the Fantaisie. It always seemed to me, when I saw the forest scene in " Siegfried," for instance, or the moonlight scene outside Siegmund's hut in the " Valkyr " (the Munich and Bayreuth settings, by the way), that Wagner had copied bits from the charming valley leading to the Fantaisie, and that the dancing effect of the sunlight falling through the foliage upon the greensward, in the second act of "Siegfried," came from watching similar effects under the grand old elms of the Hermitage.

But this was imagination only. " Siegfried " was thought out and written in Switzerland long before Wagner went to Bayreuth, and as a matter of fact, the poetic sketches, the scenes, and the principal leading musical themes or motives— that is, the whole poetical, dramatic, and scenic structure of his great music dramas—were invented while he was writing the poetic sketch of his works, and in the case of the Ring, nearly a quarter of a century before he completed them in the musical form in which they are to-day published.

Wagner could not draw inspiration from nothing. His music came from his subject and his words; he did not write the words after he had invented his musical ideas. The greatest trouble that Richard Wagner ever had in his life, perhaps, was after he had accepted the commission to

THE MARKET PLACE IN BAYREUTH WHERE WAGNER CONCEIVED THE IDEA OF A MOTIVE FOR HIS CENTENNIAL MARCH.

write the Centennial March for the Ladies' Committee of the Philadelphia Exhibition. He wandered, puzzled to distraction, about the streets of Bayreuth for days and days, trying to think of a leading phrase on which to build his musical structure. He often expressed his regret that he had undertaken the commission. He would never have done so, indeed, had not his financial needs been so pressing, for Wagner was always terribly in debt, and remained so until the day of his death. Finally, at the end of two weeks, he appeared in radiant mood among his friends.

"I have it," he exclaimed. "What?" was the inquiry. "My musical idea for *die Americaner*." It was a phrase from some of the older composers, which constantly recurs in the Centennial March. Wagner admitted frankly that he borrowed the leading theme which he used in the March. Now, had the Ladies' Committee taken the trouble to write out a musical sketch of the history of the United States, illustrated it with characteristic songs, airs, and marches, and sent some one with this to explain to the Master at Bayreuth, we might to-day have had a Centennial March of which we should be proud. What different results Wagner achieved in the Huldigangs March, written in honor of King Ludwig II., and in the Kaiser March, written after the conclusion of the Franco-German war, in which he utilizes the melody of Luther's grand old choral, "Ein feste Burg," in such an effective manner.

The visitor to Bayreuth will not leave the old capital without going to Villa Wahnfried, which Wagner had built from his own designs, where he lived, and whither he was brought home for burial. Villa Wahnfried is a plain, symmetrical, admirably arranged structure, of dignified architecture, and is surrounded by a few acres of garden and grounds, laid out with taste and simplicity. Over the portal is a large encaustic picture, beneath which is inscribed, in conspicuous capitals, the name which the composer gave to his home—"Wahnfried." There are two lines of German, in gold letters, on either side of the name, explaining to us the meaning of the somewhat curious designation:

Hier wo mein Wahn　　　　　　Sey dieses Haus
　　　　　WAHNFRIED
　Frieden fand—　　　　　　　Von mir genannt.

"Wahnfried," translated, means, literally, "Peace to the Ideal," and the entire inscription reads in English thus: "Here, where I found the fulfilment of my Ideal—Wahnfried—So shall this house be named." Over the entrance is a large allegorical fresco by Krauss, of Dresden, with the figure of Wotan, as representing German mythology; two female figures, "Tragedy" and "Lyric Art," and young Siegfried, as sym-

WAHNFRIED.

bolizing the "art-work," the music of the future. That fresco has really an historical interest. The central figure is that of Betz, the Berlin basso, in the character of Wotan; the female figure representing Tragedy is a portrait of Mme. Schroeder-Devrient, whose dramatic impersonations had a great influence upon Wagner's career; and the other figure, representing Lyric Art, is an idealized portrait of Mme. Cosima Wagner herself; while the boy is the portrait of Wagner's little son, Siegfried, costumed like the operatic hero.

The interior of "Villa Wahnfried" is fitted up with great elegance. We enter a broad, spacious hall, something like the central apartment of an old Pompeiian dwelling, from which all the rooms of the house are approached. It is lighted through a colored glass window in the roof; a gallery encircles it at about two-thirds of the height from the ground, and leads to the sleeping apartments of the family. It can be used as a general reception- or smoking-room, and contains a large grand piano and small tables for coffee. Around about it are miniature copies of Professor Echter's frescoes, representing scenes from the music-drama of the "Ring," and tastefully placed marble statuettes by Professor Zumbusch, of Vienna, representing the various heroic figures of Wagner's operatic creations—Tannhäuser, Lohengrin, Van der Decken, Siegfried, Tristan, and Walther von Stolzing. The lobby leads into the large *salon*, which is at the same time the composer's study and sanctum, and consequently of considerable interest to us. It occupies the entire width of the house and receives its light through a large bay-window, in the centre of which a door takes one to the lawn and garden in front. The large *salon* was Wagner's study and library; handsome cases, filled with well-selected, and in some cases very rare, books extend completely around the room. The collection of musical literature is very rich. The master's own operas and music-dramas have a wide shelf to themselves, close to the works of Beethoven, Haydn, Mozart, Händel, Gluck, Weber, Palestrina, Halévy, Liszt, and other composers. Above the bookcases are portraits of King Ludwig, the philosopher Schopenhauer, Franz Liszt, Beethoven, Wagner, and Madame Wagner. A large grand piano occupies one corner of the *salon*. Tables and stands are loaded with albums, photographs, presentation

AN EVENING WITH WAGNER.

1, Frau Lilli Lehmann. 2, Rubenstein. 3, Hans Richter. 4, R. Wagner. 5, Frau Materna. 6, Betz. 7, Wilhelmj. 8, Niemann. 9, Brandt.

copies of books, art-treasures, presents, plants, and flowers. There are marble busts of King Ludwig, of Wagner himself, of Madame Wagner, and on one of the tables lies the death-mask of Wagner's great master—Beethoven. In the midst of all this artistic confusion, at a large marble table near the window, and seated in a comfortable armchair, Wagner composed the "Goetterdaemmerung," the last music drama of the "Ring of the Nibelung."

When I was in Bayreuth the Villa Wahnfried was filled with the glad laughter of children— four girls and a boy, ranging from four to fifteen or sixteen years of age—Senta, Elisabeth, Eva, Isolde, and the little boy Siegfried. The latter only was Wagner's own child. The former were born to Cosima Liszt while she was still the wife of Von Bulow. Siegfried was then a manly little fellow, and the very image of the composer. Madame Wagner bore a striking resemblance to her father, Franz Liszt. To her, to Franz Liszt, and King Ludwig the world owes much. Without them, Wagner's ideals would probably have remained unfulfilled. We only need to read the lately published correspondence between Liszt and Wagner to find the most interesting revelations in this respect. Without Liszt's devotion and assistance, which were given before King Ludwig's, Wagner would perhaps never have had the courage to proceed with the musical completion of the Ring, and it is sure that without the splendid support given to him by Mme. Cosima, he would have wearied on his herculean task, and have sunk under the burden he had imposed upon himself.

Mrs. Cosima Wagner is a woman of great intellectual force. She was not only wife to Wagner, but his most ardent admirer, supporter, and worshipper. For many years before his death she was of great assistance to the poet-composer, transacting most of his business and attending to his correspondence, receiving his visitors, and taking care that he should not be unnecessarily disturbed in his artistic life. And in return Wagner idolized her. A writer from Bayreuth recently described her as she is now, in words that seem to demand a place here. "The woman whose hand I grasped, whose lofty, calm, marvellously winsome imperiousness, and impassiveness, and her supreme loyalty to her husband, converted all enemies to friends. Her shining faith in the dead master's deification

WAGNER.
(Last picture taken—1883.)

and in her own final reunion with him, would transform the whole world to Wagnerian disciples could it be brought within her influence. This one woman was as necessary as life itself to the complete development of Wagner's purpose to create for the world an absolutely new standard in lyric music.

"Probably now sixty years of age, 'Madame Cosima' is a head taller than was the poet-composer. Quaint and odd in dress, spare and gaunt in figure, the startling effect is heightened by the longest and scrawniest neck ever connecting woman's head and frame. She is as sallow as was her venerable father. Deep but phenomenally bright and piercing eyes gleam out under heavy brows. Her nose is long and hawked. Her mouth is large, with lips firmly set, with an expression of unconquerable will-power; and all this is intensified by iron-gray hair hooding the sides of the face almost to the chin, which is then gathered in a huge knot at the top of the head. There never lived so homely and yet so fascinating a man as was Liszt, whose grotesque face I have studied in parlors and at pianos by the hour. Cosima Wagner is his prototype in woman. I believe her to be what Wagner ever insisted she was, the most intellectual woman in Germany. Not this alone. Her intellectuality was even surpassed by her matchless devotion. It did not make her his enemy. It made her make him. No flattery ever tempted her into the weakness of vanity regarding her own majestic part in what the world got from Wagner. Hence, and because of this royal abnegation only, she must ever be known as luminously as he who would not have gained immortality without just that power from her and just that abnegation which devoutly holds to this hour. "No, the world is wrong," she said. "It was all his mighty genius. I could help but little." Then, with great spirit, this remarkable assertion: "It is the eternal principle that the male shall create; that the female shall nurture. Few women ever created. They were 'derelicts,' wandering forces, when so striving. Had these known the master-power of mated genius in man, their contribution to the world's good would have been infinitely greater!" Cosima Wagner not only gave her own magnificent powers to Wagner, but she made Liszt his endless and all-powerful slave. These two tremendous forces, with access to a king's treasury, gave him power to realize his idea fully; a fortune no composer before him had ever possessed."

Close beside Villa Wahnfried, in the garden at the side of the house, Richard Wagner lies buried. It is one of the many graves in

WAGNER'S BIRTHPLACE IN LEIPSIC.

Bayreuth to which pilgrimages will be made for generations to come. There are two in the cemetery, one the immense bowlder or granite block which marks the last resting place of Jean Paul Frederick Richter, the other of Franz Liszt, who died in Bayreuth, cared for tenderly by his daughter, in whose arms he breathed his last.

That Wagner was born in Leipsic, on May 22, 1813, is brought to mind by the fact that over the house in which he first saw the light a memorial tablet has just been placed recording the fact that: "In this house was born Richard Wagner." His death day is also brought to mind by the announcement that the eighth anniversary of the composer's death day (February 13, 1883, was duly remembered and commemorated at Venice, where he died, by a concert in which only excerpts from Tannhäuser, Lohengrin, and Rienzi were performed; when "the work of the orchestra is said to have been excellent and the audience listened with rapt attention."

Wagner died in the Vendramin Palace, which looks out upon the Grand Canal. After the Parsifal performances of 1882, the poet-composer had gone to Italy to recuperate from the exhaustion caused by his arduous labors in Bayreuth. The cause of death was heart failure. On the Monday before he had visited his bankers, from whom he received money for the purpose of making an excursion with his little son

Siegfried. The next day, Tuesday, he remained in his study until two in the afternoon, when he suddenly came out and complained to the servant "that he did not know what was amiss with him." At three o'clock dinner was announced. The family sat down to the table. Suddenly the composer rose from his seat ex-

PALAZZO VENDRAMIN, VENICE.

claiming, "Mir ist sehr schlecht" (I feel very ill), and sank senseless to the floor. Mrs. Wagner and her daughters, with the gondolier Luigi, raised him up and carried him to his work-room. At half-past four the great composer was dead. He had had premonitions of death. A few weeks before, he conducted the production of his Symphony in the Venice Conservatory. As he laid down the bâton he said, sadly, "I shall never conduct again." "Why?" someone asked him. "Because I shall soon die." On the Ash Wednesday he bade Luigi take him in his gondola to San Michele, the cemetery-island of Venice. When he was getting out he said to Luigi, "How long will it be before I shall find my last resting-place?—"'Wie lange noch—und ich werde auch mein stilles Plaetzchen finden?'"

Five days after death, the remains of the poet-composer, accompanied by Mme. Cosima, his children, and representatives from the whole musical world, arrived in Bayreuth. As mourners, were representatives from the Wagner Societies of Berlin, Vienna, Frankfort, Mannheim, Rotterdam, Brussels, Dresden, Leipsic, Dusseldorf, Munich, Prague, Venice, Bremen, Brunswick. Every theatre of importance, every Wagner society, every art-loving German prince, the King of Bavaria foremost among them all, had sent their musical and military representatives. Wreaths and garlands filled two capacious wagons. The richest were sent by King Ludwig and the city of Venice. To the sorrowful strains of the Siegfried funeral march the open hearse, drawn by four black steeds, left the railway station. The crowd uncovered, and strong men wept, for "a great man was dead and the world was poorer."

There were few dry eyes. "I never beheld such a child-like display of unaffected grief," wrote an eye-witness. "To-day I saw men

THE FUNERAL PROCESSION THROUGH BAYREUTH.

whose names are as household words in the artistic world of Europe, sobbing and embracing each other in sympathetic sorrow before the bier." The procession formed, and, amid the tolling of bells, slowly moved away through the quaint old streets of Bayreuth. First came a detachment of the fire brigade, followed by two death heralds and a military band; then the two wagon-loads of evergreen wreaths and immortelles; then the hearse, flanked by torch-bearers, and followed by the clergy; then the representatives of the King of Bavaria, with Siegfried, the son of the dead composer, and the family relatives; then the various musical and artistic mourners and deputations, officers of the garri-

WAGNER'S GRAVE.

son, the municipality, and a band playing the Funeral March. Half an hour brought the procession to Villa Wahnfried. The coffin was borne to the grave by eight men who had been of Wagner's most intimate friends and disciples in life, prominent among them being Albert Niemann and Hans Richter. Brief religious services were held, and the coffin was lowered into its vault. The big Newfoundland dog, that used to follow his master about in the old days, on those wanderings around Bayreuth, fawned upon the various members of the sorrowing family, as if he really understood their grief. The bright day was ending. Darkness was beginning to fall, and as each mourner left the tomb he plucked a laurel leaf or a snow-drop from the wreaths that lay piled around in affectionate memory of the world's greatest genius.

So was Wagner borne to his last resting-place.

www.ingramcontent.com/pod-product-compliance
Lightning Source LLC
Chambersburg PA
CBHW020152170426
43199CB00010B/998